32

D0743488

International Standard Banking Practice (ISBP)
for the examination of documents under documentary credits

Approved by the ICC Banking Commission

The world business organization

International standard
banking practice (ISBP) fo

Published in January 2003 by

ICC PUBLISHING S.A.
International Chamber of Commerce
The world business organization
38 Cours Albert 1er
75008 Paris, France

ICC Publication No. 645
ISBN 92 842 1314 2

FOREWORD

The publication *International Standard Banking Practice for the Examination of Documents under Documentary Letters of Credit* is the product of two and a half years of work by a task force of the ICC Banking Commission. It was approved by the full Commission at its meeting in Rome in October 2002, at which time, the Commission voted to make it an official document of the ICC.

The ISBP, as it is more commonly called, is a practical complement to UCP 500, ICC's universally used rules on documentary credits. The ISBP does not amend the UCP. It explains, in explicit detail, how the rules are to be applied on a day-to-day basis. As such, It fills a needed gap between the general principles announced in the rules and the daily work of the documentary credit practitioner.

The task force that developed the ISBP was meticulous in seeking to document international practice in the field. It started by asking ICC national committees and members to send checklists on how documents were examined in their banks. Some 39 national committees and a substantial number of individual banks responded. Culling these comments required 14 task force meetings and four different drafts before the ISBP was finally in a shape to be approved.

The task force deserves considerable credit for having proceeded so carefully. The object of the exercise was to document *international* standard banking practice for the examination of documents under the UCP; it was *not* to report on individual country practices that may differ in some way from the norm. The UCP was created to bring uniformity to a field in which individual practices often differed, to the detriment of documentary practitioners in all countries.

By using the ISBP, document checkers can bring their practices in line with those followed by their colleagues worldwide. The result should be a significant reduction in the number of documents refused for discrepancies on first presentation.

The task force that laboured so long to bring this important text to fruition deserves special mention. Their names are listed below:

Co-Chairs
- Ole Malmqvist, Danske Bank, Denmark
- Donald R. Smith, Citibank NA, US

Members
- Professor James E. Byrne, Institute for International Banking Law and Practice, US
- Gary Collyer, ABN Amro Bank, UK
- Haluk Erdemol, Akbank, Turkey
- Merike Gramer, Svenska Handelsbanken, Sweden
- Wolfgang Heiter, Deutsche Bank, Germany
- Heinz Hertl, Bank Austria, Austria
- Reinhard Längerich, Nordea Bank, Denmark
- Jean-Pierre Mattout, France Telecom, France
- Neville Sawyer, Barclays Bank plc, UK
- Soh Chee Seng, Association of Banks, Singapore

Maria Livanos Cattaui
Secretary General
International Chamber of Commerce
Paris, France
December 2002

CONTENTS

Ocean/marine bills of lading (covering port-to-port shipment)

Charter party bills of lading

Multimodal transport documents

Air transport documents

Road, rail or inland waterway transport documents

Insurance documents

Certificates of origin

ICC at a glance   55

Selected ICC publications   57

INTRODUCTION

At its May 2000 meeting the Commission on Banking Technique and Practice of the International Chamber of Commerce (ICC Banking Commission) established a task force to document international standard banking practice for the examination of documents presented under documentary credits issued subject to the *Uniform Customs and Practice for Documentary Credits*, the International Chamber of Commerce's Publication No. 500 (UCP).

The international standard banking practices documented in this publication are consistent with the UCP and the Opinions and Decisions of the ICC Banking Commission. This document does not amend UCP. It explains how the practices articulated in the UCP are to be applied by documentary practitioners. It is, of course, recognized that the law in some countries may compel a different practice than that stated here.

No single publication can anticipate all the terms or the documents that may be used in connection with documentary credits or their interpretation under the UCP and the standard practice it reflects. However, the task force preparing this publication has endeavoured to cover terms commonly seen on a day-to-day basis and the documents most often presented under documentary credits.

It should be noted that any term in a documentary credit which modifies or affects the applicability of a provision of the UCP may also have an impact on international standard banking practice. Therefore, in considering the practices described in this publication, parties must take into account any term in a documentary credit that expressly excludes or modifies a provision in an article of the UCP. This principle is implicit throughout this publication, whether or not stated, but it is sometimes expressly repeated for purposes of emphasis or for illustration. Where examples are given, these are solely for the purpose of illustration and are not exhaustive.

This publication reflects international standard banking practice for all parties to a documentary credit. Since applicants' obligations, rights, and remedies depend upon their undertaking with the issuing bank, the performance of the underlying transaction, and the time-liness of any objection under applicable law and practice, appli-cants should not assume that they may rely on these provisions in order to excuse their obligations to reimburse the issuing bank. The incorporation of this publication into the terms of a documentary credit should be discouraged, as the requirement to follow agreed practices is implicit in the UCP.

Because this publication reflects current documentary credit practice as provided by ICC national committees and individual ICC members, it will be of considerable use in the formulation of any future revision of the UCP.

PRELIMINARY CONSIDERATIONS

The application and issuance of the credit

1. The terms of a credit are independent of the underlying trans-
    action even if a credit expressly refers to that transaction. To
    avoid unnecessary costs, delays, and disputes in the exam-
    ination of documents, however, the applicant and beneficiary
    should carefully consider which documents should be required,
    by whom they should be produced, and the time frame for
    presentation.

2. The applicant bears the risk of any ambiguity in its instructions
    to issue or amend a credit. Unless expressly stated otherwise,
    a request to issue or amend a credit authorizes an issuer to
    supplement or develop the terms in a manner necessary or
    desirable to permit the use of the credit.

3. The applicant should be aware that the UCP contains Articles
    such as Articles 13, 20, 21, 23, 24, 26, 27, 28, 39, 40, 46 and
    47 that define terms in a manner that may produce unexpected
    results unless the applicant fully acquaints itself with these
    provisions. For example, a credit requiring presentation of a
    marine bill of lading and containing a prohibition against
    transhipment will, in most cases, have to exclude UCP sub-
    Article 23(d) to make the prohibition against transhipment
    effective.

4. A credit should not require presentation of documents that
    are to be issued and/or countersigned by the applicant. If a
    credit is issued including such terms, the beneficiary must
    either seek amendment or comply with them and bear the
    risk of failure to do so.

5. Many of the problems that arise at the examination stage could
    be avoided or resolved by careful attention to detail in the
    underlying transaction, the credit application, and issuance
    of the credit as discussed.

GENERAL PRINCIPLES

Abbreviations

6. The use of generally accepted abbreviations, for example "Ltd" instead of "Limited", "Int'l" instead of "International", "Co." instead of "Company", "kgs" or "kos" instead of "kilos", "Ind." instead of "Industry", "mfr" instead of "manufacturer" or "mt" instead of "metric tons" – or vice versa – does not make a document discrepant.

7. Virgules (slash marks "/") may have different meanings, and unless apparent in the context used, should not be used as a substitute for a word.

Certifications and declarations

8. A certification, declaration or the like may either be a separate document or contained within another document as required by the credit. If the certification or declaration appears in another document which is signed and dated, any certification or declaration appearing on that document does not require a separate signature or date if the certification or declaration appears to have been given by the same entity that issued and signed the document.

Corrections and alterations

9. Corrections and alterations of information or data in documents, other than documents created by the beneficiary, must appear to be authenticated by the party who issued the document or by a party authorized by the issuer to do so. Corrections and alterations in documents which have been legalized, visaed, or the like, must appear to be authenticated by the party who legalized, visaed, etc., the document. The authentication must show by whom the authentication has been made and include that party's signature or initials. If the authentication appears to have been made by a party other than the issuer of the document, the authentication must clearly show in which capacity that party has authenticated the correction or alteration.

10. Corrections and alterations in documents issued by the beneficiary itself, except drafts, which have not been legalized, visaed or the like, need not be authenticated. See also "Drafts and calculation of maturity date".

11. The use of multiple type styles or font sizes or handwriting in the same document does not, by itself, signify a correction or alteration.

12. Where a document contains more than one correction or alteration, either each correction must be authenticated separately or one authentication must be linked to all corrections in an appropriate way. For example, if the document shows three corrections numbered 1, 2 and 3, one statement such as "Correction numbers 1, 2 and 3 above authorized by XXX" or similar, will satisfy the requirement for authentication.

Dates

13. Drafts, transport documents and insurance documents must be dated even if a credit does not expressly so require. A requirement that a document, other than those mentioned above, be dated, may be satisfied by reference in the document to the date of another document forming part of the same presentation (e.g., where a shipping certificate is issued which states "date as per bill of lading number xxx" or similar terms). Although it is expected that a required certificate or declaration in a separate document be dated, its compliance will depend on the type of certification or declaration that has been requested, its required wording, and the wording that appears within it. Whether other documents require dating will depend on the nature and content of the document in question.

14. Any document, including a certificate of analysis, inspection certificate and pre-shipment inspection certificate, may be dated after the date of shipment. However, if a credit requires a document evidencing a pre-shipment event (e.g., pre-shipment inspection certificate), the document must, either by its title or content, indicate that the event (e.g., inspection) took place prior to or on the date of shipment. A requirement for an "inspection certificate" does not constitute a requirement to evidence a pre-shipment event. Documents must not indicate that they were issued after the date they are presented.

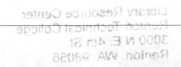

15. A document indicating a date of preparation and a later date of signing is deemed to be issued on the date of signing.

16. The rule for the latest date for presentation in sub-Article 43(a) of UCP applies only to presentations that are required to contain one or more original transport documents. Transport documents are those covered by UCP Articles 23-29. In any event, documents must be presented not later than the expiry date of the credit.

17. Phrases often used to signify timo on either side of a date or event:

a) "within 2 days after" indicates a period from the date of the event until two days after the event.

b) "not later than 2 days after" does not indicate a period, only a latest date. If an advice must not be dated prior to a specific date, the credit must so state.

c) "at least 2 days before" indicates that something must take place not later than two days before an event. There is no limit as to how early it may take place.

d) "within 2 days of" indicates a period two days prior to the event until two days after the event.

18. The term "within" when used in connection with a date excludes that date in the calculation of the period.

19. Dates may be expressed in different formats, e.g., the 12th of November 2003 could be expressed as 12 Nov 03, 12Nov03, 12.11.2003, 12.11.03, 2003.11.12, 11.12.03, 121103, etc. Provided that the date intended can be determined from the document or from other documents included in the presentation, any of these formats are acceptable. To avoid confusion it is recommended that the name of the month should be used instead of the number.

Documents for which the UCP Transport Articles do not apply

20. Some documents commonly used in relation to the transportation of goods, e.g., Delivery Order, Forwarder's Certificate of Receipt, Forwarder's Certificate of Shipment, Forwarder's Certificate of Transport, Forwarder's Cargo Receipt and Mate's Receipt do not reflect a contract of carriage and are not transport documents as defined in UCP Articles 23 through 29. As such, UCP Article 43 would not apply to these documents. Therefore, these documents will be examined in the same manner as other documents for which there are no specific provisions in the UCP, i.e., under UCP Article 21. In any event, documents must be presented not later than the expiry date of the credit.

21. Copies of transport documents are not transport documents for the purpose of UCP Articles 23-29 and 43. The UCP Transport Articles apply where there are original transport documents presented. Where a credit allows for the presentation of a copy(ies) rather than an original(s), the credit must explicitly state the details to be shown. Where copies (non-negotiable) are presented, they need not evidence signature, dates, etc.

Expressions not defined in UCP

22. Expressions such as "shipping documents", "stale documents acceptable", "third party documents acceptable", and "exporting country" should not be used as they are not defined in UCP. If used in a credit, their meaning should be made apparent. If not, they have the following meaning under international standard banking practice:

a) "shipping documents" – all documents (not only transport documents), except drafts, required by the credit.

b) "stale documents acceptable" – documents presented later than 21 days after the date of shipment are acceptable as long as they are presented within the validity of the credit.

c) "third party documents acceptable" – all documents, excluding drafts but including invoices, may be issued by a party other than the beneficiary. If the issuing bank's intent is that the transport document(s) may show a shipper other than the beneficiary, the clause is not necessary because it is already permitted by UCP sub-Article 31(iii).

d) "exporting country" – the country where the beneficiary is domiciled, and/or the country of origin of the goods, and/or the country of receipt by the carrier and/or the country from which shipment or dispatch is made.

23. Words and phrases such as "prompt", "immediately", "as soon as possible", and the like should not be used in any context. If they are used banks will disregard them.

Inconsistency in the documents

24. Documents presented under a credit must not appear to be inconsistent with each other. The requirement is not that the data content be identical, merely that the documents not be inconsistent.

Issuer of documents

25. If a credit indicates that a document is to be issued by a named person or entity, this condition is satisfied if the document appears to be issued by the named person or entity. It may appear to be issued by a named person or entity by use of its letterhead, or, if there is no letterhead, the document appears to have been completed and/or signed by, or on behalf of, the named person or entity.

Language

26. Under international standard banking practice, it is expected that documents issued by the beneficiary will be in the language of the credit. When a credit states that documents in two or more languages are acceptable, a nominated bank may, in its advice of the credit, limit the number of acceptable languages as a condition of its engagement in the credit or confirmation.

Mathematical calculations

27. Detailed mathematical calculations in documents will not be checked by banks. Banks are only obliged to check total values against the credit and other required documents.

Misspellings or typing errors

28. Misspellings or typing errors that do not affect the meaning of a word or the sentence in which it occurs, do not make a document discrepant. For example, a description of the merchandise as "mashine" instead of "machine", "fountan pen" instead of "fountain pen" or "modle" instead of "model" would not make the document discrepant. However, a description as "model 123" instead of "model 321" would not be regarded as a typing error and would constitute a discrepancy.

Multiple pages and attachments or riders

29. Unless the credit or a document provides otherwise, pages which are physically bound together, sequentially numbered or contain internal cross references, however named or entitled, are to be examined as one document, even if some of the pages are regarded as an attachment. Where a document consists of more than one page, it must be possible to determine that the pages are part of the same document.

30. If a signature and/or endorsement is required to be on a document consisting of more than one page, the signature is normally placed on the first or last page of the document, but unless the credit or the document itself indicates where a signature or endorsement is to appear, the signature or endorsement may appear anywhere on the document.

Originals and copies

31. Documents issued in more than one original may be marked "Original", "Duplicate", "Triplicate", "First Original", "Second Original", etc. None of these markings will disqualify a document as an original.

32. Each required document must be presented in at least one original, unless the credit allows for presentation of documents as copies. The number of originals to be presented must be at least the number required by the credit, the UCP, or, where the document itself states how many originals have been issued, the number stated on the document.

33. It can sometimes be difficult to determine from the wording of a credit whether it requires an original or a copy, and to determine whether that requirement is satisfied by an original or a copy. For example, where the credit requires:

a) "Invoice", "One Invoice" or "Invoice in 1 copy", it will be understood to be a requirement for an original invoice.

b) "Invoice in 4 copies", it will be satisfied by the presentation of at least one original and the remaining number as copies of an invoice.

c) "One copy of Invoice", it will be satisfied by presentation of a copy of an invoice. However, it is standard banking practice to accept an original instead of a copy in this construction.

34. Where an original would not be accepted in lieu of a copy, the credit must prohibit an original, e g , "photocopy of invoice – original document not acceptable in lieu of photocopy", or the like.

35. The ICC Banking Commission Policy Statement, document 470/871(Rev), titled "The determination of an "Original" document in the context of UCP sub-Article 20(b)" is recommended for further guidance on originals versus copies.

Shipping marks

36. The purpose of a shipping mark is to enable identification of a box, bag or package. If a credit specifies the details of a shipping mark, the document(s) mentioning the marks must show these details, but additional information is acceptable provided it is not inconsistent with the credit terms.

37. Shipping marks contained in some documents often include information in excess of what would normally be considered "shipping marks", and could include information such as the type of goods, warnings as to the handling of fragile goods, net and/or gross weight of the goods, etc. The fact that some documents show such additional information, while others do not, is not a discrepancy.

38. Transport documents covering containerized goods will sometimes only show a container number under the heading "Shipping marks". Other documents that show a detailed marking will not be considered to be inconsistent for that reason.

Signatures

39. Even if not stated in the credit, drafts, certificates and declarations by their nature require a signature. Transport documents and insurance documents must be signed in accordance with the provisions of the UCP.

40. The fact that a document has a box or space for a signature does not necessarily mean that such box or space must be completed with a signature. For example, banks do not require a signature in the area titled "Signature of shipper or their agent", or similar phrases, commonly found on transport documents such as air waybills or road transport documents. If a document on its face requires a signature for its validity (e.g., "This document is not valid unless signed", or similar terms), it must be signed.

41. A signature need not be handwritten. Facsimile signatures, perforated signatures, stamps, symbols (such as chops) or any electronic or mechanical means of authentication are sufficient. However, a photocopy of a signed document does not qualify as a signed original document, nor does a signed document transmitted through a fax-machine, absent an original signature. A requirement for a document to be "signed and stamped", or a similar requirement, is also fulfilled by a signature and the name of the party typed, or stamped, or handwritten, etc.

42. A signature on a company's letterhead paper will be taken to be the signature of that company, unless otherwise stated. The company's name need not be repeated next to the signature.

Title of documents and combined documents

43. Documents may be titled as called for in the credit, bear a similar title, or be untitled. For example, a credit requirement for a "Packing List" may also be satisfied by a document containing packing details whether titled "Packing Note", "Packing and Weight List", etc., or an untitled document. The content of a document must appear to fulfill the function of the required document.

44. Documents listed in a credit should be presented as separate documents. If a credit requires a packing list and a weight list, such requirement will be satisfied by presentation of two separate documents, or by presentation of two original copies of a combined packing and weight list, provided such document states both packing and weight details.

DRAFTS AND CALCULATION OF MATURITY DATE

Tenor

45. The tenor must be in accordance with the terms of the credit.

a) If a draft is drawn at a tenor other than sight, or other than a certain period after sight, it must be possible to establish the maturity date from the data in the draft itself.

b) As an example of where it is possible to establish a maturity date from the data in the draft, if a credit calls for drafts at a tenor 60 days after the bill of lading date, where the date of the bill of lading is 12 May 2002, the tenor could be indicated on the draft in one of the following ways:

   i. "60 days after bill of lading date 12 May 2002", or

   ii. "60 days after 12 May 2002", or

   iii. "60 days after bill of lading date" and elsewhere on the face of the draft state "bill of lading date 12 May 2002", or

   iv. "60 days date" on a draft dated the same day as the date of the bill of lading,or

   v. "11 July 2002", i.e., 60 days after the bill of lading date.

c) If the tenor refers to xxx days after the bill of lading date, the on board date is deemed to be the bill of lading date even if the on board date is prior to or later than the date of issuance of the bill of lading.

d) The UCP provides no guidance where the words "from" and "after" are used to determine maturity dates of drafts. Reference to "from" and "after" in the UCP refers solely to date terminology for periods of shipment. Where the word "from" is used to establish the maturity date, international standard banking practice would exclude the date mentioned, unless the credit specifically provides that "from" is considered to include the date mentioned. Therefore, for the purposes of determining the maturity date of a time draft, the words "from" and "after" have the same effect. Calculation of the maturity commences the day following the date of the document, shipment, or other event, i.e., 10 days after or from March 1 is March 11.

e) If a bill of lading showing more than one on board notation is presented under a credit which requires drafts to be drawn, for example, at 60 days after or from bill of lading date, and the goods according to both or all on board notations were shipped from ports within a permitted geographical area or region, the earliest of these on board dates will be used for calculation of the maturity date. Example: the credit requires shipment from European port and the bill of lading evidences on board vessel "A" from Dublin August 16, and on board vessel "B" from Rotterdam August 18. The draft should reflect 60 days from the earliest on board date in a European port, i.e., August 16.

f) If a credit requires drafts to be drawn, for example, at 60 days after or from bill of lading date, and more than one set of bills of lading are presented under one draft, the date of the last bill of lading will be used for the calculation of the maturity date.

46. While the examples refer to bill of lading dates, the same principles apply to all transport documents.

Maturity date

47. If a draft states a maturity date by using an actual date, the date must have been calculated in accordance with the requirements of the credit.

48. For drafts drawn "at XXX days sight", the maturity date is established as follows:

a) in the case of complying documents, or in the case of non-complying documents where the drawee bank has not provided a refusal of documents, the maturity date will be XXX days after the date of receipt of documents by the drawee bank.

b) in the case of non-complying documents where the drawee bank has provided a notice of refusal of documents and subsequent approval, at the latest XXX days after the date of acceptance of the draft by the drawee bank. The date of acceptance of the draft must be no later than the date of approval of the documents.

49. In all cases the drawee bank must advise the maturity date to the presenter. The calculation of tenor and maturity dates, as shown above, would also apply to credits designated as being available by deferred payment, i.e., where there is no requirement for a draft to be presented by the beneficiary.

Banking days, grace days, delays in remittance

50. Payment must be available in immediately available funds on the due date at the place where the draft or documents are payable, provided such due date is a banking day in that place. If the due date is a non-banking day, payment will be due on the first banking day following the due date unless the credit states otherwise. Delays in the remittance of funds, such as grace days, the time it takes to remit funds, etc., must not be in addition to the stated or agreed due date as defined by the draft or documents.

Endorsement

51. The draft must be endorsed, if necessary.

Amounts

52. The amount in words must accurately reflect the amount in figures if both are shown, and indicate the currency, as stated in the credit.

53. The amount must agree with that of the invoice, unless otherwise stated in the credit or as a result of UCP sub-Article 37(b).

How the draft is drawn

54. The draft must be drawn on the party stated in the credit.

55. The draft must be drawn by the beneficiary.

Drafts on the applicant

56. Credits should not be issued requiring that drafts be drawn on the applicant. If a credit calls for drafts to be drawn on the applicant, banks must consider such drafts as additional documents to be reviewed in accordance with UCP Article 21.

Corrections and alterations

57. Corrections and alterations on a draft, if any, must appear to have been authenticated by the drawer.

58. In some countries draft(s) showing corrections and alterations are not acceptable even with the drawer's authentication. Issuing banks in such countries should make a statement in the credit to the effect that no correction or alteration must appear in the draft(s).

INVOICES

Definition of invoice

59. A credit requiring an "invoice" without further definition will be satisfied by any type of invoice presented (commercial invoice, customs invoice, tax invoice, final invoice, consular invoice, etc.). However, invoices identified as "provisional", "pro-forma", or the like are not acceptable unless specifically authorized in the credit. When a credit requires presentation of a commercial invoice, a document titled "invoice" will be acceptable.

Name and address

60. An invoice must appear on its face to have been issued by the beneficiary named in the credit. Telex or fax numbers, etc., forming part of the address, need not be present, or, if stated, need not be identical to that in the credit.

61. An invoice must be made out in the name of the applicant. Telex or fax numbers, etc., forming part of the address, need not be present, or, if stated, need not be identical to that in the credit.

Description of the goods and other general issues related to invoices

62. The description of the goods in the invoice must correspond with the description in the credit. There is no requirement for a mirror image. For example, details of the goods may be stated in a number of areas within the invoice which, when collated together, represents a description of the goods corresponding to that in the credit.

63. The goods description in an invoice must reflect what goods have been actually shipped. For example, where there are two types of goods shown in the credit, such as 10 trucks and 5 tractors, an invoice that reflects only shipment of 4 trucks would be acceptable provided the credit does not prohibit

partial shipment. An invoice showing the entire goods description as stated in the credit, then stating what has actually
been shipped, is also acceptable.

64. An invoice must evidence the value of the goods shipped.
Unit price(s), if any, and currency shown in the invoice must
agree with that shown in the credit. The invoice must show
any discounts or deductions required in the credit. The invoice
may also show a deduction covering advance payment,
discount, etc., not stated in the credit.

65. If a trade term is part of the goods description in the credit, or
stated in connection with the amount, the invoice must state
the trade term specified, and if the description provides the
source of the trade term, the same source must be identified
(e.g., a credit term "CIF Singapore Incoterms 2000" would
not be satisfied by "CIF Singapore Incoterms", etc.). Charges
and costs must be included within the value shown against
the stated trade term in the credit and invoice. Any charges
and costs shown beyond this value are not allowed.

66. Unless required by the credit, an invoice need not be signed
or dated.

67. The quantity of merchandise, weights, and measurements
shown on the invoice must be not inconsistent with the same
quantities appearing on other documents.

68. An invoice must not show:
   a) over-shipment (except as provided in UCP sub-Article
   39(b)), or

   b) merchandise not called for in the credit (including samples,
   advertising materials, etc.) even if stated to be free of charge.

69. The quantity of the goods required in the credit may vary within
a tolerance of +/- 5%. This does not apply if a credit stipulates
that the quantity must not be exceeded or reduced, or if a
credit stipulates the quantity in terms of a stated number of
packing units or individual items. A variance of up to +5% in
the goods quantity does not allow the amount of the drawing
to exceed the amount of the credit.

70. If partial shipments are prohibited, a tolerance of 5% less in the invoice amount is acceptable, provided that the quantity is shipped in full and that any unit price, if stated in the credit, has not been reduced. If no quantity is stated in the credit, the invoice will be considered to cover the full quantity.

71. The required number of originals and copies must be presented.

72. If a credit calls for instalment shipments, each shipment must be in accordance with the instalment schedule.

OCEAN/MARINE BILLS OF LADING (COVERING PORT-TO-PORT SHIPMENT)

Application of UCP Article 23

73. If a credit requires presentation of a transport document covering a port-to-port shipment, UCP Article 23 is applicable.

74. If a credit requires presentation of a "marine" or "ocean" transport document, UCP Article 23 applies. A transport document need not use the term "marine" or "ocean" in order to comply with UCP Article 23 provided that it covers a port-to-port shipment.

Full set of originals

75. A UCP Article 23 transport document must indicate the number of originals that have been issued. Transport documents marked "First Original", "Second Original", "Third Original", "Original", "Duplicate", "Triplicate", etc., or similar expressions are all originals. Bills of lading need not be marked "original" to be acceptable as an original bill of lading. See section 3.1 of ICC Publication 470/871Rev., 20 July 1999, "The determination of an "Original" document in the context of UCP 500 sub-Article 20(b)".

Signing of bills of lading

76. Original bills of lading must bear a signature in the form described in UCP sub-Article 20(b) and the name of the carrier must appear on the face of the bill of lading, identified as the carrier.

    a) If an agent signs a bill of lading on behalf of a carrier, the agent must be identified as agent, and must identify the carrier on whose behalf it is signing, unless the carrier has been identified elsewhere on the face of the bill of lading.

b) If the master (captain) signs the bill of lading, the signature of the master (captain) must be identified as "master" ("captain"). In this event, the name of the master (captain) need not be stated.

c) If an agent signs the bill of lading on behalf of the master (captain), the agent must be identified as agent and the name of the master (captain) on whose behalf it is signing must be stated.

77. If a credit states "Freight Forwarder's Bill of Lading is acceptable" or uses a similar phrase, then the bill of lading may be signed by a freight forwarder in the capacity of a freight forwarder, without the need to identify itself as carrier or agent for the named carrier. It is not necessary to show the name of the carrier.

On board notations

78. If a pre-printed "Shipped on board" bill of lading is presented, its issuance date will be deemed to be the date of shipment unless it bears a separate dated on board notation, in which event the date of the on board notation will be deemed to be the date of shipment whether or not the on board date is before or after the issuance date of the bill of lading.

79. "Shipped in apparent good order", "Laden on board", "clean on board" or other phrases incorporating words such as "shipped" or "on board" have the same effect as "Shipped on board".

Ports of loading and ports of discharge

80. While the named port of loading, as required by the credit, should appear in the port of loading field within the bill of lading, it may instead be stated in the field headed "Place of receipt" or the like, if it is clear that the goods were transported from that place of receipt by vessel, and provided there is an on board notation evidencing that the goods were loaded on that vessel at the port stated under "Place of receipt" or like term.

81. While the named port of discharge, as required by the credit, should appear in the port of discharge field within the bill of lading, it may be stated in the field headed "Place of final destination" or the like if it is clear that the goods were to be transported to that place of final destination by vessel, and provided there is a notation evidencing that the port of discharge is that stated under "Place of final destination" or like term.

82. If a Container Yard (CY) or Container Freight Station (CFS) is stated as the place of receipt and that place is the same as the stated port of loading (e.g., Place of Receipt: Hong Kong CY; Port of Loading: Hong Kong), these places are deemed to be the same, and therefore the specification of the port of loading and the name of the vessel in the "on board" notation are not necessary.

83. If a credit gives a geographical area or range of ports of loading and/or discharge (e.g., "Any European Port"), the bill of lading must indicate the actual port of loading and/or discharge, which must be within the geographical area or range quoted.

Consignee, order party, shipper and endorsement, notify party

84. If a credit requires a bill of lading to show that the goods are consigned to a named party, e.g., "consigned to Bank X" (a "straight" consignment), rather than "to order" or "to order of Bank X", the bill of lading must not contain words such as "to order" or "to order of" that precede the name of that named party, whether typed or pre-printed. Likewise, if a credit requires the goods to be consigned "to order" or "to order of" a named party, the bill of lading must not show that the goods are consigned straight to the named party.

85. If a bill of lading is issued to order, or to order of the shipper, it must be endorsed by the shipper. An endorsement indicating that it is made for or on behalf of the shipper is acceptable.

86. If a credit does not state a notify party(ies), the respective field on the bill of lading may be left blank or completed in any manner.

Transhipment and partial shipment

87. Transhipment is the unloading and reloading of goods from one vessel to another during the course of ocean carriage from the port of loading to the port of discharge stipulated in the credit. If it does not occur between these two ports, unloading and reloading is not considered to be transhipment.

88. Although transhipment may be prohibited, UCP sub-Article 23(d) nonetheless permits transhipment under certain circumstances. If, however, a credit prohibits transhipment and excludes UCP sub-Articles 23(d)(i) and (ii), a bill of lading that indicates on its face that transhipment will or may take place will be considered discrepant.

89. If a credit prohibits partial shipments, and more than one set of original bills of lading are presented covering shipment from one or more ports of loading (as specifically allowed, or within a given range, in the credit), such documents are acceptable provided that they cover the shipment of goods on the same vessel and same journey and are destined for the same port of discharge. In the event that more than one set of bills of lading are presented, and incorporate different dates of shipment, the latest of these dates of shipment will be taken for the calculation of any presentation period and must fall on or before the latest shipment date specified in the credit. Shipment on more than one vessel is a partial shipment, even if the vessels leave on the same day for the same destination.

Clean bills of lading

90. Clauses or notations on bills of lading which expressly declare a defective condition of the goods and/or packaging are not acceptable. Clauses or notations which do not expressly declare a defective condition of the goods and/or packaging (e.g., "packaging may not be sufficient for the sea journey") do not constitute a discrepancy. A statement that the packaging "is not sufficient for the sea journey" would not be acceptable.

91. The word "clean" need not appear on a bill of lading even though the credit may require a "clean on board bill of lading" or one marked "clean on board".

92. If the word "clean" appears on a bill of lading and has been deleted, the bill of lading will not be deemed to be claused or unclean unless It specifically boars a clause or notation declaring that the goods or packaging are defective.

Goods description

93. A goods description in the bill of lading may be shown in general terms not inconsistent with that stated in the credit.

Corrections and alterations

94. Corrections and alterations on a bill of lading must be authenticated. Such authentication must appear to have been made by the carrier, master (captain), or any of their agents (who may be different from the agent that may have issued or signed it), provided they are identified as an agent of the carrier or the master (captain).

95. Non-negotiable copies of bills of lading do not need to include any signature on, or authentication of any alterations or corrections that may have been made on the original.

Freight and additional costs

96. If a credit requires that a bill of lading show that freight has been paid or is payable at destination, the bill of lading must be marked accordingly.

97. Applicants and issuing banks should be specific in stating the requirements of documents to show whether freight is to be prepaid or collected.

98. If a credit states that costs additional to freight are not acceptable, a bill of lading must not indicate that costs additional to the freight have been or will be incurred. Such indication may be by express reference to additional costs or by the use of shipment terms which refer to costs associated with the loading or unloading of goods, such as Free In (FI), Free Out (FO), Free In and Out (FIO) and Free In and Out Stowed (FIOS). A reference in the transport document to costs which may be levied as a result of a delay in unloading the goods or after the goods have been unloaded, e.g., costs covering the late return of containers, is not considered to be an indication of additional costs in this context.

Goods covered by more than one bill of lading

99. If a bill of lading states that the goods in a container are covered by that bill of lading plus one or more other bills of lading, or words of similar effect, this means that the entire container is to be surrendered to the consignee and therefore all bills of lading related to that container must be presented in order for the container to be released. Such a bill of lading is not acceptable unless all the bills of lading form part of the same presentation under the same credit.

CHARTER PARTY BILLS OF LADING

Application of UCP Article 25

100. If a credit requires presentation of a charter party bill of lading covering a port-to-port shipment, UCP Article 25 is applicable. A transport document containing any indication that it is subject to a charter party is a charter party bill of lading under UCP Article 25.

101. If a credit requires presentation of a charter party bill of lading, then a marine transport document presented containing an indication that it is subject to a charter party must fulfill the requirements of UCP Article 25.

Full set of originals

102. A UCP Article 25 transport document must indicate the number of originals that have been issued. Transport documents marked "First Original", "Second Original", "Third Original", "Original", "Duplicate", "Triplicate", etc., or similar expressions are all originals. Charter party bills of lading need not be marked "original" to be acceptable under a credit. See section 3.1 of ICC Publication 470/871 Rev. 29, July 1999, "The determination of an 'Original' document in the context of UCP 500 sub-Article 20(b)".

Signing of charter party bills of lading

103. Original charter party bills of lading must bear a signature in the form described in UCP sub-Article 20(b).

a) If the master (captain) or owner signs the charter party bill of lading, the signature of the master (captain) or owner must be identified as "master" ("captain") or "owner".

b) If an agent signs the charter party bill of lading on behalf of the master (captain) or owner, the agent must be identified as agent and the name of the master (captain) or owner on whose behalf it is signing is required to be stated.

On board notations

104. If a pre-printed "Shipped on board" charter party bill of lading is presented, its issuance date will be deemed to be the date of shipment unless it bears an on board notation, in which event the date of the on board notation will be deemed to be the date of shipment whether or not the on board date is before or after the issuance date of the document.

105. "Shipped in apparent good order", "Laden on board", "clean on board" or other phrases incorporating words such as "shipped" or "on board" have the same effect as "shipped on board".

Ports of loading and ports of discharge

106. If a credit gives a geographical area or range of ports of loading and/or discharge (e.g., "Any European Port"), the charter party bill of lading must indicate the actual port(s) of loading, which must be within the geographical area or range indicated but may show the geographical area or range of ports as the port of discharge.

Consignee, order party, shipper and endorsement, notify party

107. If a credit requires a charter party bill of lading be consigned to a named party (e.g., "consigned to Bank X", rather than "to order" or "to order of Bank X") (a "straight" consignment), the charter party bill of lading must not contain words such as "to order" or "to order of" that precede the name of that named party, whether typed or pre-printed. Likewise, if a credit requires a charter party bill of lading to be consigned "to order" or "to order of" a named party, the bill of lading must not be consigned straight to the named party.

108. If a charter party bill of lading is issued to order, or to order of the shipper, it must be endorsed by the shipper. An endorsement indicating that it is made for or on behalf of the shipper is acceptable.

109. If a credit does not state a notify party(ies), the respective field on the charter party bill of lading may be left blank or completed in any manner.

Partial shipment

110. If a credit prohibits partial shipments, and more than one set of original charter party bills of lading are presented covering shipment from one or more ports of loading (as specifically allowed, or within a given range, in the credit), such documents are acceptable, provided that they cover the shipment of goods on the same vessel and same journey and are destined for the same port of discharge, range of ports or geographical area. In the event that more than one set of charter party bills of lading are presented, and incorporate different dates of shipment, the latest of these dates of shipment will be taken for the calculation of any presentation period and must fall on or before the latest shipment date specified in the credit. Shipment on more than one vessel is a partial shipment, even if the vessels leave on the same day for the same destination.

Clean charter party bills of lading

111. Clauses or notations on charter party bills of lading which expressly declare a defective condition of the goods and/or packaging are not acceptable. Clauses or notations that do not expressly declare a defective condition of the goods and/or packaging (e.g., "packaging may not be sufficient for the sea journey") do not constitute a discrepancy. A statement that the packaging "is not sufficient for the sea journey" would not be acceptable.

112. The word "clean" need not appear on a charter party bill of lading even though the credit may require a "clean on board charter party bill of lading" or one marked "clean on board".

113. If the word "clean" appears on a charter party bill of lading and is deleted, the charter party bill of lading will not be deemed to be claused or unclean unless it specifically bears a clause or notation declaring that the goods or packaging are defective.

Goods description

114. A goods description in charter party bills of lading may be shown in general terms not inconsistent with that stated in the credit.

Corrections and alterations

115. Corrections and alterations on charter party bills of lading must be authenticated. Such authentication must appear to have been made by the owner, master (captain), or any of their agents (who may be different from the agent that may have issued or signed it), provided they are identified as an agent of the owner or the master (captain).

116. Non-negotiable copies of charter party bills of lading do not need to include any signature on, or authentication for any alterations or corrections that may have been made on the original.

Freight and additional costs

117. If a credit requires that a charter party bill of lading show that freight has been paid or is payable at destination, the charter party bill of lading must be marked accordingly.

118. Applicants and issuing banks should be specific in stating the requirements of documents to show whether freight is to be prepaid or collected.

119. If a credit states that costs additional to freight are not acceptable, a charter party bill of lading must not indicate that costs additional to the freight have been or will be incurred. Such indication may be by express reference to additional costs or by the use of shipment terms which refer to costs associated with the loading or unloading of goods, such as Free In (FI), Free Out (FO), Free In and Out (FIO) and Free In and Out Stowed (FIOS). A reference in the transport document to costs which may be levied as a result of a delay in unloading the goods, or after the goods have been unloaded, is not considered to be an indication of additional costs in this context.

MULTIMODAL TRANSPORT DOCUMENTS

Application of UCP Article 26

120. If a credit requires presentation of a transport document covering transportation utilizing at least two modes of transport, and if the transport document clearly shows that it covers a shipment from the place of taking in charge and/or port, airport or place of loading to the place of final destination mentioned in the credit, UCP Article 26 is applicable. In such circumstances, a multimodal transport document must not indicate that shipment or dispatch has been effected by only one mode of transport, but it may be silent regarding the modes of transport utilized.

121. In all places where the term multimodal transport document is used within this document, it also includes the term combined transport document. A document need not be titled "Multimodal transport document" or "Combined transport document" to be acceptable under UCP Article 26, even if such expressions are used in the credit.

Full set of originals

122. A UCP Article 26 transport document must indicate the number of originals that have been issued. Transport documents marked "First Original", "Second Original", "Third Original", "Original", "Duplicate", "Triplicate", etc., or similar expressions are all originals. Multimodal transport documents need not be marked "original" to be acceptable under a credit. See ICC Banking Commission Decision on Original Documents (section 3.1) dated 12 July 1990.

Signing of multimodal transport documents

123. Original multimodal transport documents must bear a signature in the form described in UCP sub-Article 20(b) and the name of the carrier or multimodal transport operator must appear on the face of the multimodal transport document, identified as the carrier or multimodal transport operator.

a) If an agent signs a multimodal transport document on behalf of the carrier or multimodal transport operator, the agent must be identified as agent, and must identify on whose behalf it is signing, unless the carrier or multimodal transport operator has been identified elsewhere on the face of the multimodal transport document.

b) If the master (captain) signs the multimodal transport document, the signature of the master (captain) must be identified as "master" ("captain"). In this event, the name of the master (captain) need not be stated.

c) If an agent signs the multimodal transport document on behalf of the master (captain), the agent must be identified as agent and the name of the master (captain) on whose behalf it is signing must be stated.

124. If a credit states "Freight Forwarder's Multimodal transport document is acceptable" or uses a similar phrase, then the multimodal transport document may be signed by a freight forwarder in the capacity of a freight forwarder, without the need to identify itself as carrier or multimodal transport operator or their agent. It is not necessary to show the name of the carrier or multimodal transport operator.

On board notations

125. The issuance date of a multimodal transport document will be deemed to be the date of dispatch, taking in charge or loading on board unless it bears a separate dated notation evidencing dispatch, taking in charge or loading on board from the location required by the credit, in which event the date of the notation will be deemed to be the date of shipment whether or not the date is before or after the issuance date of the document.

126. "Shipped in apparent good order", "Laden on board", "clean on board" or other phrases incorporating words such as "shipped" or "on board" have the same effect as "Shipped on board".

Place of taking in charge, dispatch, loading on board and destination

127. If a credit gives a geographical range for the place of taking in charge, dispatch, loading on board and destination (e.g., "Any European Port"), the multimodal transport document must indicate the actual place of taking in charge, dispatch, loading on board and destination, which must be within the geographical area or range quoted.

Consignee, order party, shipper and endorsement, notify party

128. If a credit requires that a multimodal transport document to show that the goods are consigned to a named party, e.g., "consigned to Bank X" (a "straight" consignment), rather than "to order" or "to order of Bank X", the multimodal transport document must not contain words such as "to order" and "to order of" that precede the name of that named party, whether typed or pre-printed. Likewise, if a credit requires the goods to be consigned "to order" or "to order of" a named party, the multimodal transport document must not show that the goods are consigned straight to the named party.

129. If a multimodal transport document is issued to order, or to order of the shipper, it must be endorsed by the shipper. An endorsement indicating that it is made for or on behalf of the shipper is acceptable.

130. If a credit does not stipulate a notify party(ies), the respective field on the multimodal transport document may be left blank or completed in any manner.

Transhipment and partial shipment

131. In a multimodal transport shipment, transhipment will occur, i.e., the unloading and reloading of goods from one mode of transport to another during the course of the journey from the point of taking in charge, dispatch or loading on board, to the final destination stipulated in the credit. Should transhipment be prohibited, banks will accept a multimodal transport document evidencing that transhipment has occurred provided the entire journey is covered by one and the same multimodal transport document.

132. If a credit prohibits partial shipments and more than one set of original multimodal transport documents are presented covering shipment, dispatch or taking in charge from one or more points of origin (as specifically allowed or within a given range in the credit), such documents are acceptable provided that they cover the movement of goods on the same means of conveyance and same journey and are destined for the same destination. In the event that more than one set of multi-modal transport documents are presented, and if they incorporate different dates of shipment, dispatch or taking in charge, the latest of these dates will be taken for the calcul-ation of any presentation period, and such date must fall on or before any latest date of shipment, dispatch or taking in charge specified in the credit.

133. Shipment on more than one means of conveyance (more than one truck (lorry), vessel, aircraft, etc.) is a partial shipment, even if such means of conveyance leave on the same day for the same destination.

Clean multimodal transport documents

134. Clauses or notations on multimodal transport documents that expressly declare a defective condition of the goods and/or packaging are not acceptable. Clauses or notations that do not expressly declare a defective condition of the goods and/or packaging (e.g., "packaging may not be sufficient for the journey") do not constitute a discrepancy. A statement that the packaging "is not sufficient for the journey" would not be acceptable.

135. The word "clean" need not appear on a multimodal transport document even though the credit may require a "clean on board multimodal transport document" or one marked "clean on board".

136. If the word "clean" appears on a multimodal transport document and has been deleted, the multimodal transport document will not be deemed to be claused or unclean unless it specifically bears a clause or notation declaring that the goods or packaging are defective.

Goods description

137. A goods description in the multimodal transport document may be shown in general terms not inconsistent with that stated in the credit.

Corrections and alterations

138. Corrections and alterations on a multimodal transport document must be authenticated. Such authentication must appear to have been made by the carrier, master (captain), multimodal transport operator, or any one of their agents who may be different from the agent that may have issued or signed it, provided they are identified as an agent of the carrier, master (captain) or multimodal transport operator.

139. Copies of multimodal transport documents do not need to include any signature on, or authentication of any alterations or corrections that may have been made on the original.

Freight and additional costs

140. If a credit requires that a multimodal transport document show that freight has been paid or is payable at destination, the multimodal transport document must be marked accordingly.

141. Applicants and issuing banks should be specific in stating the requirements of documents to show whether freight is to be prepaid or collected.

142. If a credit states that costs additional to freight are not acceptable, a multimodal transport document must not indicate that costs additional to the freight have been or will be incurred. Such indication may be by express reference to additional costs or by the use of shipment terms which refer to costs associated with the loading or unloading of goods, such as Free In (FI), Free Out (FO), Free In and Out (FIO) and Free In and Out Stowed (FIOS). A reference in the transport document to costs which may be levied as a result of a delay in unloading the goods or after the goods have been unloaded is not considered to be an indication of additional costs in this context.

Goods covered by more than one multimodal transport document

143. If a multimodal transport document states that the goods in a container are covered by that multimodal transport document plus one or more other multimodal transport documents or words of similar effect, this means that the entire container is to be surrendered to the consignee and therefore all multimodal transport documents related to that container must be presented in order for the container to be released. Such a multimodal transport document is not acceptable unless all the multimodal transport documents are presented in the same presentation under the same credit.

AIR TRANSPORT DOCUMENTS

Application of UCP Article 27

144. If a credit requires presentation of a transport document covering an airport-to-airport shipment, UCP Article 27 is applicable.

145. If a credit required presentation of an "air waybill" or "air consignment note" or similar, UCP Article 27 applies. An air transport document need not use these terms in order to comply with UCP Article 27 provided that it covers an airport-to-airport shipment.

Original air transport documents

146. The air transport document must appear, from the face of the document, to be the "Original for Consignor/Shipper". A requirement for a full set of originals is satisfied by the presentation of a document indicating that it is the original for consignor/shipper.

Signing of air transport documents

147. An original air transport document must bear a signature in the form described in UCP sub-Article 20(b) and the name of the carrier must appear on the face of the air transport document, identified as the carrier. If an agent signs an air transport document on behalf of a carrier, the agent must be identified as agent, and must identify the carrier on whose behalf it is signing, unless the carrier has been identified elsewhere on the face of the air transport document.

148. If a credit states "House air waybill is acceptable" or "Freight Forwarder's air waybill is acceptable" or uses a similar phrase, then the air transport document may be signed by a freight forwarder in the capacity of a freight forwarder, without the need to identify itself as a carrier or agent for a named carrier. It is not necessary to show the name of the carrier.

Goods accepted for carriage, date of shipment, and requirement for an actual date of dispatch

149. An air transport document must indicate that the goods have been accepted for carriage.

150. If a credit indicates that an actual date of dispatch must appear on the air transport document, the document must contain a separate notation that provides this information. This date of dispatch will be considered as the date of shipment. Information contained in the boxes typically titled "For Carrier Use Only" will not be considered for determining the actual date of dispatch.

151. If no actual date of dispatch is required by the credit to be shown on the document, the date of issuance of an air transport document will be deemed to be the date of dispatch, even if the document shows a flight date and/or a flight number in the box marked "For Carrier Use Only" or similar expression. If the actual flight date is shown as a separate notation, but is not required by the credit, it will be disregarded in determining the date of shipment.

Airports of departure and destination

152. Air transport documents must indicate the airport of departure and airport of destination as stated in the credit. The identification of airports by the use of IATA codes instead of writing out the name in full (e.g., LHR instead of London Heathrow) is not a discrepancy.

153. If a credit gives a geographical area or range of airports of departure and/or destination (e.g., "Any European Airport"), the air transport document must indicate the actual airport of departure and/or destination, which must be within that geographical area or range quoted.

Consignee, order party and notify party

154. Air transport documents should not be issued "to order" or "to order of" a named party because they are not documents of title. Even if a credit calls for an air transport document made out "to order" or "to order of" a named party, a document presented showing goods consigned to that party, without mention of "to order" or "to order of", is acceptable.

155. If a credit does not state a notify party(ies), the respective field on the air transport document may be left blank or completed in any manner.

Transhipment and partial shipment

156. Transhipment is the unloading and reloading of goods from one aircraft to another during the course of carriage from the airport of departure to the airport of destination stipulated in the credit. If it does not occur between these two airports, unloading and reloading is not considered to be transhipment.

157. Although transhipment may be prohibited, UCP sub-Article 27(c) nonetheless permits transhipment provided the entire carriage is covered by one and the same air transport document.

158. If a credit prohibits partial shipments, and more than one air transport document is presented covering dispatch from one or more airports of departure (as specifically allowed, or within a given range, in the credit), such documents are acceptable, provided that they cover the dispatch of goods on the same aircraft and same flight, and are destined for the same airport of destination. In the event that more than one air transport document is presented incorporating different dates of shipment, the latest of these dates of shipment will be taken for the calculation of any presentation period and such date must fall on or before the latest shipment date specified in the credit.

159. Shipment on more than one aircraft is a partial shipment, even if the aircraft leave on the same day for the same destination.

Clean air transport documents

160. Clauses or notations on an air transport document which expressly declare a defective condition of the goods, and/or packaging are not acceptable. Clauses or notations on the air transport document which do not expressly declare a defective condition of the goods and/or packaging (e.g., "packaging may not be sufficient for the air journey") do not constitute a discrepancy. Statements that the packaging "is not sufficient for the air journey" would not be acceptable.

161. The word "clean" need not appear on the air transport document even though the credit may require a "clean air waybill" or one marked "clean on board".

162. If the word "clean" appears on an air transport document and has been deleted, the air transport document will not be deemed to be claused or unclean unless it specifically bears a clause or notation declaring that the goods or packaging are defective.

Goods description

163. A goods description in an air transport document may be shown in general terms not inconsistent with that stated in the credit.

Corrections and alterations

164. Corrections and alterations on air transport documents must be authenticated. Such authentication must appear to have been made by the carrier or any of its agents (who may be different from the agent that may have issued or signed it), provided it is identified as an agent of the carrier.

165. Copies of air transport documents do not need to include any signature of the carrier or agent (or shipper even if required by the credit to appear on the original air transport document), nor any authentication of any alterations or corrections that may have been made on the original.

Freight and additional costs

166. If a credit requires that an air transport document show that freight has been paid or is payable at destination, the air transport document must be marked accordingly.

167. Applicants and issuing banks should be specific in stating the requirements of documents to show whether freight is to be prepaid or collected.

168. If a credit states that costs additional to freight are not acceptable, an air transport document must not indicate that costs additional to the freight have been or will be incurred. Such indication may be by express reference to additional costs or by the use of shipment terms that refer to costs associated with the loading or unloading of goods. A reference in the transport document to costs which may be levied as a result of a delay in unloading the goods or after the goods have been unloaded is not considered an indication of additional costs in this context.

169. Air transport documents often have separate boxes which, by their pre-printed headings, indicate that they are for freight charges "prepaid" and for freight charges "to collect", respectively. A requirement in a credit for an air transport document to show that freight has been prepaid will be fulfilled by a statement of the freight charges under the heading "Freight Prepaid", or a similar expression or indication, and a requirement that an air transport document show that freight has to be collected will be fulfilled by a statement of the freight charges under the heading "Freight to Collect", or a similar expression or indication.

ROAD, RAIL OR INLAND WATERWAY TRANSPORT DOCUMENTS

Application of UCP Article 28

170. If a credit requires presentation of a transport document covering movement by road, rail or inland waterway, UCP Article 28 is applicable.

Original and duplicate of road, rail or inland waterway transport documents

171. If a credit requires a road, rail or inland waterway transport document, the transport document presented will be accepted as an original whether or not it is marked as an original. A road transport document must show that it is the copy meant for the shipper or consignor or bear no marking indicating for whom the document has been prepared. With respect to rail waybills, the practice of many railway companies is to provide the shipper or consignor with only a duplicate (often a carbon copy) duly authenticated by the railway company's stamp. Such a duplicate will be accepted as an original.

Carrier and signing of road, rail or inland waterway transport documents

172. The term "carrier" need not appear at the signature line provided the transport document appears to be signed by the carrier, or an agent on behalf of the carrier, if the carrier is otherwise identified as the "carrier" on the face of the transport document. International standard banking practice is to accept a railway bill evidencing date stamp by the railway station of departure without showing the name of the carrier or a named agent signing for or on behalf of the carrier. (UCP sub-Article 28(a)(i)).

173. The term "carrier" used in UCP Article 28 includes terms in transport documents such as "issuing carrier", "actual carrier", "succeeding carrier", and "contracting carrier".

174. Any signature, authentication, reception stamp, or other indication of receipt on the transport document must appear to be made either by:

    a) the carrier, identified as the carrier, or

    b) a named agent signing for or on behalf of the carrier, and indicating the name and capacity of the carrier on whose behalf that agent is signing.

Order party and notify party

175. Transport documents which are not documents of title should not be issued "to order" or "to order of" a named party. Even if a credit calls for a transport document which is not a document of title to be made out "to order" or "to order of" a named party, such a document, showing goods consigned to that party, without mention of "to order" or "to order of", is acceptable.

176. If a credit does not stipulate a notify party(ies), the respective field on the transport document may be left blank or completed in any manner.

Partial shipment

177. Shipment on more than one means of conveyance (more than one truck (lorry), train, vessel, etc.) is a partial shipment, even if such means of conveyance leave on the same day for the same destination.

Goods description

178. A goods description in the transport document may be shown in general terms not inconsistent with that stated in the credit.

Corrections and alterations

179. Corrections and alterations on an UCP Article 28 transport document must be authenticated. Such authentication must appear to have been made by the carrier, or any one of their named agents, who may be different from the agent that may have issued or signed it, provided they are identified as an agent of the carrier.

180. Copies of UCP Article 28 transport documents do not need to include any signature on, or authentication of any alterations or corrections that may have been made on the original.

Freight and additional costs

181. If a credit requires that a UCP Article 28 transport document show that freight has been paid or is payable at destination, the transport document must be marked accordingly.

182. Applicants and issuing banks should be specific in stating the requirements of documents to show whether freight is to be prepaid or collected.

INSURANCE DOCUMENTS

Application of UCP Articles 34-36

183. If a credit requires presentation of an insurance document, UCP Articles 34 through 36 are applicable.

Issuers of insurance documents

184. Insurance documents must appear on their face to have been issued and signed by insurance companies or underwriters or their agents. If required on the face of the insurance document or in accordance with the credit terms, all originals must appear to have been countersigned.

185. An insurance document is acceptable if issued on an insurance broker's stationery, provided the insurance document has been signed by the insurance company or its agent, or by the underwriter or its agent A broker may sign as agent for the named insurance company or the named underwriter.

Risks to be covered

186. The insurance document must cover the risks defined in the credit. If a credit is explicit with regard to risks to be covered, there must be no exclusions referenced in the document with respect to those risks. If a credit requires "all risks" coverage, this is satisfied by the presentation of an insurance document evidencing any "all risks" clause or notation, even if it is stated that certain risks are excluded. An insurance document indicating that it covers Institute Cargo Clauses (A) satisfies a condition in a credit calling for an "all risks" clause or notation.

187. Insurance covering the same risk for the same shipment must be covered under one document unless the insurance documents for partial cover each clearly reflect, by percentage or otherwise, the value of each insurer's cover and that each insurer will bear their share of the liability severally and without pre-conditions relating to any other insurance cover that may have been effected for that shipment. An insurance document that clearly reflects, by percentage or otherwise, the share of liability that each insurer will bear is acceptable provided joint liability is declared, or the leading insurer states that it bears 100% of the covered risk.

188. The insurance document must show that risks are covered at least between the point of shipment, dispatch or taking in charge and the point of discharge or final destination as required by the credit.

Dates

189. Insurance documents must not bear a date of issuance which is later than the date of loading on board or dispatch or taking in charge of the goods (as applicable) at the place stated in the credit, unless it appears from the insurance document that the cover is effective at the latest from the date of loading on board or dispatch or taking in charge (as applicable) of the goods at the place stated in the credit.

190. An insurance document that incorporates an expiry date must clearly indicate that such expiry date relates to the latest date that loading on board or dispatch or taking in charge of the goods (as applicable) is to occur, as opposed to an expiry date for the presentation of any claims thereunder.

Currency and amount

191. An insurance document must be issued in the currency of and, as a minimum, for the amount required by the credit. If a credit does not state a minimum percentage amount, then the minimum insurance amount must be 110% of the CIF value, or 110% of CIP value, as determined by the amounts reflected on the invoice or any other required document. A requirement for "Insurance for 110%", or the like, is deemed to be the minimum amount of insurance coverage required. The UCP does not provide for any maximum percentage.

192. If a credit requires the insurance cover to be irrespective of percentage, the insurance document must not contain a clause stating that the insurance cover is subject to a franchise or an excess deductible.

193. If it is apparent from the credit or from the documents that the final invoice amount only represents a certain part of the gross value of the goods (e.g., due to discounts, pre-payments or the like, or because part of the value of the goods is to be paid at a later date), the calculation of insurance cover must be based on the full gross value of the goods.

Insured party and endorsement

194. An insurance document must be in the form as required by the credit and, where necessary, be endorsed by the party to whose order claims are payable. A document issued to bearer is acceptable where the credit requires an insurance document endorsed in blank and vice versa.

195. If a credit is silent as to the insured party, an insurance document evidencing that claims are payable to the order of the shipper or beneficiary would not be acceptable unless endorsed. An insurance document should be issued or endorsed so that the right to receive payment under it passes upon, or prior to, the release of the documents.

CERTIFICATES OF ORIGIN

Basic requirement

196. A requirement for a certificate of origin will be satisfied by the presentation of a signed, dated document that certifies to the origin of the goods.

Issuers of certificates of origin

197. A certificate of origin must be issued by the party stated in the credit. However, if a credit requires a certificate of origin to be issued by the beneficiary, the exporter or the manufacturer, a document issued by a chamber of commerce will be deemed acceptable provided it clearly identifies the beneficiary, the exporter or the manufacturer as the case may be. If a credit does not state who is to issue the certificate, then a document issued by any party, including the beneficiary, is acceptable.

Contents of certificates of origin

198. The certificate of origin must appear to relate to the invoiced goods. The goods description in the certificate of origin may be shown in general terms not inconsistent with that stated in the credit or by any other reference indicating a relation to the goods in a required document.

199. Consignee information, if shown, must not be inconsistent with the consignee information in the transport document. However, if a credit requires a transport document to be issued "to order", "to the order of shipper", "to order of the issuing bank", or "consigned to the issuing bank", the certificate of origin may show the applicant of the credit, or another party named therein, as consignee. If a credit has been transferred, the name of the first beneficiary as consignee would also be acceptable.

200. The certificate of origin may show the consignor or exporter as a party other than the beneficiary of the credit or the shipper on the transport document.

ICC AT A GLANCE

ICC is the world business organization. It is the only representative body that speaks with authority on behalf of enterprises from all sectors in every part of the world.

ICC's purpose is to promote an open international trade and investment system and the market economy worldwide. It makes rules that govern the conduct of business across borders. It provides essential services, foremost among them the ICC International Court of Arbitration, the world's leading institution of its kind.

Within a year of the creation of the United Nations, ICC was granted consultative status at the highest level with the UN and its specialized agencies. Today ICC is the preferred partner of international and regional organizations whenever decisions have to be made on global issues of importance to business.

Business leaders and experts drawn from ICC membership establish the business stance on broad issues of trade and investment policy as well as on vital technical or sectoral subjects. These include financial services, information technologies, telecommunications, marketing ethics, the environment, transportation, competition law and intellectual property, among others.

ICC was founded in 1919 by a handful of far-sighted business leaders. Today it groups thousands of member companies and associations from over 130 countries. National committees in all major capitals coordinate with their membership to address the concerns of the business community and to put across to their governments the business views formulated by ICC.

Some ICC Services
- The ICC International Court of Arbitration (Paris)
- The ICC International Centre for Expertise (Paris)
- The ICC World Chambers Federation (Paris)
- The ICC Institute of World Business Law (Paris)
- The ICC Centre for Maritime Co-operation (London)

- ICC Commercial Crime Services (London), grouping:
  - The ICC Counterfeiting Intelligence Bureau
  - The ICC Commercial Crime Bureau
  - The ICC International Maritime Bureau

ICC Publishing S.A.

ICC Publishing, the publishing subsidiary of ICC, produces and sells the works of ICC commissions and experts as well as guides and corporate handbooks on a range of business topics. Some 100 titles – designed for anyone interested in international trade – are available from ICC Publishing.

For more detailed information on ICC publications and on the above-listed activities, and to receive the programme of ICC events, please contact ICC Headquarters in Paris or the ICC national committee in your country.

HOW TO BECOME MEMBER OF ICC
There are two possible ways of becoming a member
of the International Chamber of Commerce: either through
(1) affiliation with an ICC national committee or group or through
(2) direct membership where no national committee
or group exists.

SELECTED ICC PUBLICATIONS

Banking and trade finance

DCInsight –the quarterly information source in international trade finance and business trends

This ICC newsletter, published four times a year, keeps the reader updated on letter of credit developments worldwide that impact directly on his or her business. Includes hard-hitting articles by ICC experts, updates on documentary credit developments from correspondents in more than thirty countries, the text of important court decisions concerning the UCP, and a calendar of seminars, conferences and other events.

E   Periodical/subscription   4 issues a year

DC-PRO – A unique tool for bankers and traders

A website developed by ICC and IMS, providing bankers and traders with information relative to documentary credits. No more leafing through reams of documents to find the L/C information needed. **DC-PRO Focus** puts it all on your screen for immediate access. **DC-PRO Mentor** (both a self-training tool and a tool for trainers) was developed to reduce training costs and improve quality simultaneously and is the only ICC approved online training in UCP 500.

For free trials and information visit ICC's website at www.iccwbo.org and click on the DC-PRO link.

ICC Banking Commission Collected Opinions 1995-2001

Edited by Gary Collyer and Ron Katz

Seven years of ICC Banking Commission Opinions can be found in this one, hardback volume, presenting answers to over 300 queries on UCP 500 and other major ICC banking rules. Collected Opinions includes the totality of the three previously published volumes on UCP 500, as well as over 125 new Opinions published here for the first time. This one key reference source includes the added advantage of a complete indexation by UCP Article, as well as a consolidated key word index.

E   575 pages   ISBN 92-842-1297-9   No. 632

ICC Guide to the eUCP

By Professor James E. Byrne and Dan Taylor

The electronic supplement to UCP 500, ICC's universally used rules on letters of credit, came into force in April 2002. Termed eUCP, this supplement is expected to revolutionize the way documentary credits are used by permitting electronic or part-electronic presentations of documents. This Guide, written by the experts who drafted the rules, provides a detailed commentary that shows how the electronic documentary credit rules work in practice.

E   236 pages   ISBN 92-842-1308-8   No. 639

Documentary Credit Law throughout the World
Edited by Professor Rolf A. Schütze and Gabriele Fontane
Laws on documentary credits in more than 35 countries can be found in this essential compilation of letter of credit laws and practice. Written by two distinguished German lawyers, the book also contains a highly useful preface linking country statutes to the UCP, the ICC rules on letters of credit used by banks worldwide. Concise, practical and packed with useful information, this is an indispensable companion volume for all documentary credit professionals.

E   152 pages   ISBN 92-842-1298-7   No. 633

ICC Guide to Bank-to-Bank Reimbursements
By Dan Taylor
A practical guide to daily operations in the area of bank-to-bank reimbursements written from the perspective of each bank party to a reimbursement transaction – the issuing bank, reimbursing bank and claiming bank. The guide provides step-by-step guidance to each party and includes detailed explanations of the principles behind each part of a reimbursement transaction.

E   80 pages   ISBN 92-842-1232-4   No. 575

A User's Handbook to the Uniform Rules for Demand Guarantees
By Dr Georges Affaki
A clear and comprehensive guide that provides a masterly presentation of the rules within the context of day-to-day bank operations. The book covers the issuance, drafting, advantages and history of the rules and explodes a number of myths that have hindered more widespread adoption of the URDG. Complete with an index to the URDG Articles, as well as a general index, this practical handbook is destined to become the essential companion to all users of the URDG.

E   208 pages   ISBN 92-842-1294-4   No. 631

Bank Guarantees in International Trade (2nd edition)
By R. Bertrams.
This fully revised edition serves to broaden the understanding of bank guarantees, emphasizing the implications and issues which can arise in the daily functioning of these legal instruments. Written from a trans-national perspective, the book has been updated and amended in the light of new developments in the law and changing patterns in practice, and accounts for the introduction of new techniques and problem areas.

E   450 pages   ISBN 92-842-1198-0   No. 547

Bills of Exchange (3rd edition)
By Dr jur. Uwe Jahn
This fully revised publication has been expanded to cover legislation in Europe, Asia and Oceania. Designed for easy reference, the clear text provides a comprehensive comparison of bills of exchange law in 67 countries and offers practical information on everyday problems in overcoming conflicts in national laws.

E   192 pages   ISBN 92-842-1250-2   No. 593

International trade

A to Z of International Trade
By Frank Reynolds
More than a dictionary, A to Z doubles as a reference book, developing terms in context and showing how they interact. Including over 2000 definitions and acronyms as well as website addresses, the dictionary's thorough cross referencing system enables you to define a word from start to finish. And A to Z takes you further, with its nine "Focus on" sections, providing well-researched introductions on air transport, bank collections, e-commerce, Incoterms, insurance, letters of credit, sales contracts, liner vessel shipping and vessel chartering. A to Z really helps you understand the language of international trade.
E   343 pages   ISBN 92-842-1277-4   No. 623

Guide to Export-Import Basics (2ⁿᵈ edition)
A fully revised edition of this ICC bestseller. Providing clear explanations of the core mechanics of trade, this guide takes a lucid look at the legal, financial, transport and e-commerce issues. Fully indexed, it also includes a handy glossary of the principal terms and abbreviations.
E   360 pages   ISBN 92-842-1309-6   No. 641

Key Words in International Trade (4ᵗʰ edition)
Over 3000 translations of the terms and abbreviations most commonly used in international law and commerce, taken from the fields of banking, transport, management, marketing, arbitration, trade, telecommunications and international organizations.
EFSDI   408 pages   ISBN 92-842-1187-5   No. 417

Transfer of Ownership in International Trade
Co-published with Kluwer Law International
The issue of ownership, although vital in international trade, is not fully covered by existing international conventions. This unique comparative study, with its detailed analysis of the legal issues arising in connection with transfer of ownership in 19 countries, allows international trade practitioners to fill the gap.
E   437 pages   ISBN 92-842-1197-2   No. 546

HOW TO OBTAIN ICC PUBLICATIONS
ICC Publications are available from ICC National Committees or Councils which exist in some 60 countries or from:

ICC PUBLISHING S.A.
38, Cours Albert 1er
75008 Paris, France
Tel: +33 1 49.53.29.23/28.89
Fax +33 1 49.53.29.02
E-mail: pub@wbo.org

ICC PUBLISHING, INC.
156 Fifth Avenue, Suite 417
New York, N.Y. 10010 (USA)
Tel: +1 212 206 1150
Fax: +1 212 633 6025
E-mail: info@iccpub.net

Visit our website at www.iccbooks.com